Write It

Writing skills for intermediate
learners of English

Learner's Book

Michael Dean

CAMBRIDGE
UNIVERSITY PRESS

For Judith and Mouse

PUBLISHED BY THE PRESS SYNDICATE OF THE UNIVERSITY OF CAMBRIDGE
The Pitt Building, Trumpington Street, Cambridge CB2 1RP, United Kingdom

CAMBRIDGE UNIVERSITY PRESS
The Edinburgh Building, Cambridge CB2 2RU, United Kingdom
40 West 20th Street, New York, NY 10011-4211, USA
10 Stamford Road, Oakleigh, Melbourne 3166, Australia

First published 1988
Sixth printing 1997

Printed in the United Kingdom at the University Press, Cambridge

ISBN 0 521 31171 3 Learner's Book
ISBN 0 521 31172 1 Teacher's Book
ISBN 0 521 32356 8 Cassette

Contents

Thanks   vi
To the learner   vii

Section 1: Brief personal writing
1 Filling in personal forms   1
2 Writing greetings cards   4
3 Writing postcards   7

Section 2: Longer personal writing
4 Writing notes   10
5 Writing letters   14
6 Letters of invitation, acceptance and refusal   18
7 Arrangements in writing   21
8 Letters of thanks   24

Section 3: Official writing – Forms, memos and letters
9 Filling in official forms   27
10 Writing memos   32
11 Writing CVs, replying to job and other advertisements   35
12 Letters of complaint   39

Section 4: Extensive writing – People, places and events
13 Describing appearance   45
14 Describing people, their jobs and their lives   49
15 Describing places   52
16 Narrative writing   57
17 Writing about public events I   60
18 Writing about public events II   63

Section 5: Extensive writing – Evaluation and opinion
19 Evaluation in writing   66
20 Opinion in writing   71

To the teacher   77
Acknowledgements   83

Thanks

I would like to thank all the schools and teachers who took part in the piloting of this book, especially Eurocentre Lee Green, Sociedade Brasileira de Cultura Inglesa in São Paulo and the Teach-In Language and Training Workshop in Rome.

Thanks to Peter Taylor for the cassette production.

The section on error correction in the Introduction to the teacher was read and commented on by several editors at CUP, by two of my colleagues at Colchester Institute, Tony Kidd and Steve Slater, and by Catherine Walter. I appreciate their time and trouble.

And to Peter Donovan, Margherita Baker, Alison Silver and Angela Wilde at CUP, thanks for the freedom and the support (I needed both).

To the learner

I want this book to do three things: I want it to help you to write to English-speaking people, both personal writing to friends and formal writing to do with jobs or advertisements or form-filling. I want it to help you pass tests or examinations in English, if you are taking any. And I want the book to make your English lessons enjoyable.

If you have any other aims in using this book then I hope the book meets these aims too.

As you see from the Contents, the book starts with brief personal writing, then longer personal writing (letter length), then official writing, then the kind of long (extensive) writing you need to communicate in depth or (sometimes) to pass exams.

I have tried to give you interesting writing tasks to do, and to help you write about yourself and your world and your opinions. I want you to use the English language to express your personality, not just study it as an abstract system.

Learning another language is difficult and so is writing textbooks. But I enjoyed writing this one, and I hope you and your teacher enjoy using it.

Welcome to the book, and good luck with your writing lessons.

Michael Dean
Colchester 1988

SECTION 1: BRIEF PERSONAL WRITING

1 Is there anything that you do not or cannot eat?

FILLING IN PERSONAL FORMS

In this unit you will practise filling in forms; the first with personal details, and the second with information you will find from reading and listening to the recording.

─── **1** ────────────────────────────────────

Here is an application form for the Royal English Language School. Work in pairs. Fill in the form for the person next to you. Ask him or her to spell his or her address in English.

Royal English Language School

Name .... Age ....

Address: Street Number ....

Street ....

Town ....

Region ....

Postcode ....

Country ....

Tel. (including dialling code) ....

Nationality ....

Occupation ....

Religion ....

Is there anything that you do not or cannot eat? ....

....

Do you smoke? ....

If you have a car or motorcycle, what is the registration number? ....

Where and for how long have you learned English? ....

....

What are your hobbies? ....

....

....

....

—— **2** ————————————————————————

Tim West is out of work. His wife, Joanna, is worried. She thinks Tim does not have enough to do. The leaflet which follows is called 'Out of work'. People who have no job pay less to go swimming, go to a multigym or play squash or tennis than people who have jobs.

Look at the leaflet and look at Tim's Timeplan below. Then fill in Tim's Timeplan from the leaflet and from information on the cassette.

MAKE A SPLASH AT YOUR LOCAL POOL

You can enjoy a cheap swim every day of the week. There are also two great special sessions to take advantage of. **WATERFUN** with giant inflatables and water games is a regular high spot. As a complete contrast **ADULTS ONLY** swimming will give you and your friends the chance to enjoy a peaceful hour in the water.

Waltham Forest Pool	**Leyton Baths***
Chingford Road, E17 5AA	High Road, E10 7AA
(527 5431)	(539 2048)

Last ticket ½hour before stated closing time.

Opening Times	At All Times
MON WED THUR	8.00am- 7.15pm
TUES FRI	8.00am- 8.15pm
SAT	8.00am- 4.00pm
SUN	8.00am-12.45pm

Opening Times	*April to September Only
MON FRI	8.00am- 7.45pm
TUES THUR	8.00am- 5.45pm
WED	8.00am- 7.30pm
SAT	8.00am- 6.00pm
SUN	CLOSED

Swim   30p
Waterfun   45p
(Tues 6-7pm, Sats 2.30-3.30pm)
Adults Only   30p
(Tues 7.30-8.30pm)

Swim   25p
Waterfun   40p
(Tues & Sats 6.30-7.30pm)
Adults Only   25p
(Weds 8-9pm)

Larkswood Pool, New Road, E4 9EZ
Spend a summer's day swimming and relaxing in the sun.
Open 10am - 6pm every day (May to September only)
Cost 35p. Last ticket 5.30pm.

Tennis

Play tennis all the year round at a court near you.

Abbots Park, E10
Coronation Gardens, E10
Higham Hill Recreation Gnd. E17
Lloyd Park, E17
Low Hall Sports Ground, E17
Ridgeway Park, E4
War Memorial Park, E4
} Available for sessions of 1 hour from 9.00am to 1 hour before park closing time Mon-Sat

Cost/Court/Hour }
Oct-March up to 12 noon FREE
Oct-March afternoon 35p
April-Sept all day 60p

LEYTONSTONE RECREATION CENTRE

Cathall Road, E11 4LA   (539 8343/4)
Play squash on one of the six courts at this superb facility. Alternatively you can take a refreshing dip in the centre's pool or enjoy a session in the multigym.

Multigym
Cost 50p
No need to book just come along
Last ticket 1 hour before stated closing time

Opening Times	At All Times
MON to FRI	9.00am- 9.00pm
SAT	9.00am- 5.00pm
SUN	9.00am-12.45pm

Squash
Cost 70p/Court/½ hour
Last booking 4.00pm
Booking in advance advisable

Opening Times	At All Times
MON to FRI	9.00am- 4.00pm

Swimming   Cost 30p

Opening Times	Morning Sessions	Afternoon Sessions
MON	Noon - 1.15pm	4.00pm-7.30pm
TUES FRI	Noon - 1.15pm	4.00pm-7.45pm
WED	Noon - 1.15pm	4.00pm-5.45pm
THUR	Noon - 1.15pm	4.00pm-8.45pm
SAT	9.00am - 3.00pm	See Waterfun
SUN	9.00am-12.30pm	2.00pm-3.45pm Summer Only

Last ticket ½ hour before stated closing time. During school holidays pool opens at 10.00am Monday-Friday and closes as above.

Waterfun and Adults only
Waterfun sessions Wednesday 6.30-7.30pm and Saturday 3.45-4.45pm. Cost 45p. Adults Only swimming Mondays and Wednesdays 8.00-9.00pm. Cost 30p.

TIM'S TIMEPLAN FOR ONE WEEK IN MARCH

Day	Time	Activity	Place	Cost
Monday				
Tuesday				
Wednesday				
Thursday				
Friday				
Saturday				
Sunday				
			Total cost per week	

2 I love you very much

WRITING GREETINGS CARDS

In this unit you will practise writing short greetings, of the sort you might write on a birthday card, for example.

—— **1** ——————————————————————

Greetings cards are very much part of the way of life in Britain, Canada, the USA and Australia.

1.1

Have you sent any greetings cards in the last year? Write the name of the person you sent the card to, your relationship to the person (friend, husband, girlfriend, etc.), and the occasion (Christmas, birthday, etc.).

1.2

Write a greeting in English to the person you sent the card to (Merry Christmas, Happy Birthday, etc.) depending on the occasion.

—— **2** ——————————————————————

Here are some pictures of greetings cards and some greetings.
Work in pairs or small groups.
Match the greetings to
the correct greetings card.
There is more than one
greeting for most of them.

1

2

a) Your English lessons were really fantastic. Please accept this present from our class.
b) Merry Christmas and a Happy New Year.
c) We send our good wishes to you both. Have another happy year.
d) Honestly, I don't know how I could have moved all that furniture without you.
e) The office will be in chaos now! Don't forget to drop in and see us from time to time.
f) Well done! I knew you'd pass first time!
g) All the best for the coming year.
h) Well done, but go slowly from now on.
i) I was very sorry to hear about this. Mary and I both send our best wishes for a speedy recovery.
j) We shall miss you. The place won't be the same without you.
k) Keep cheerful. John and I will come and visit you soon.
l) Thank you for everything, darling. I love you very much.
m) Many happy returns!

─── **3** ───────────────────────────────────

Write the greetings that you would write on a greetings card in these situations.

a) It is Christmas. You want to send a card to the person you love most in the world. You want to express your hopes for the coming year.
b) You stayed with someone in an English-speaking country and they were very kind and hospitable to you.
c) Your best friend is about to take an important examination.
d) Your best friend has just passed the important examination.
e) Some friends gave a party that you enjoyed very much.
f) It is Valentine's Day (February 14th). There is someone you know who you like very much and who you think is very attractive. Write this person a Valentine. (Valentines can be anonymous, so you do not have to say who you are.)
g) A couple you know very well have just had a baby.

3 It's a really beautiful unspoilt place

WRITING POSTCARDS

Holiday postcards are a specialized form of writing. They have their own rules.
After looking at some of the language and frameworks which people often use in
postcards, you will practise writing some.

─── **1** ───────────────────────────────────

1.1

Work in pairs. Which of these examples of writing are from a holiday postcard?

a) Last year I went to the Algarve, in the south of Portugal.
b) It's paradise here, I'm not coming back!
c) Below us, you can just see the Algarve, the southernmost tip of Portugal. We
   shall land at Faro at 1500 hours.
d) Jean has just climbed out of the swimming pool and I'm just sitting here,
   looking at the almond blossom.
e) Lots of love, Jean and Phyllis
f) I'm in Faro. Something awful's happened. For God's sake take the next plane
   out. This is urgent!
g) From our villa you can see right out over the bay and the little town of
   Albufeira in the distance; it's beautiful.
h) The local village consists of three houses, a grocery shop and four bars!
i) Dear John,
j) We are in the Algarve for two weeks.

1.2

Underline the words that tell you the other examples of writing in 1.1 are not
from a postcard.

─── **2** ───────────────────────────────────

The phrases and sentences which *are* from postcards in 1.1 go together to make
one postcard. But they are not in the right order in 1.1.
   Work in pairs. Put them in the right order and write the postcard.

—— 3 ——

Look at the postcard below. The words in each sentence and the sentences themselves are in the wrong order.

Work in pairs. Write the postcard correctly.

Dear Susie

a) our anywhere from In little is fact hotel miles.
b) in we here Well, Czechoslovakia are!
c) a unspoilt We're beautiful, in place.
d) really to looking We're forward it.
e) a on to tomorrow going We're trip Prague.
f) really country nice a It's.
g) the in office everyone to Love,

        Roger

—— 4 ——

The framework of the postcard you wrote in Exercise 3 was like this.

POSTCARD	ADDRESS
1 Greeting (optional).	_____
2 Brief description of the place where you are staying (or the hotel).	_____ _____ _____
3 Say what you are doing now or what you are going to do tomorrow.	_____ _____
4 Ending.	_____ _____

4.1.

Here is another postcard, this time from Sorrento. It uses the same framework.
Underline the word or words that do the following:

a) In the second sentence that links with 'We' in sentence one.
b) In the third sentence that links with 'hotel' in sentence two.
c) That show you the writer wants to tell you about what she is doing now.
d) That show you the writer wants to tell you she is enjoying herself.

1 Greeting   Dear Jim,

2 Place   We are in Sorrento for a fortnight. From our hotel you can see the fishermen in the famous bay (see picture). Near the hotel there is a leather factory and we bought a handbag there made of Italian leather.

3 Doing now   At the moment Dick is downstairs booking a weekend trip to Rome and I'm writing this before we go down to dinner. Spaghetti alla carbonara tonight! It's nice here but we miss you!

4 Ending   All the best,
           Sarah

4.2

Read Sarah's postcard again. Imagine she visited your home town or a place you
know well. Rewrite her Sorrento postcard from the place you know, using the
same framework.

—— **5** ————————————————————

Work in groups. Listen to the cassette, and use the noises, music and phrases on
the cassette to write postcards.

SECTION 2: LONGER PERSONAL WRITING

4 Sandra's just phoned. She's in tears
WRITING NOTES

In this unit you will practise writing short notes to different people in everyday situations.

—— 1 ——————————————

1.1

These pictures all show something that has just happened, and then somebody writing a note about what has happened. Use the pictures and the words below them to write the first sentence of each note.
Example: Roger's just phoned from the station.

This is what happened.

Note A
Peter, Roger's . . . station.

This is what happened.

Note B
Sue, Bill's car has . . . down.

This is what happened.

Note C
Darling, Tim's . . . over.

This is what happened.

Note D
Anne, we've decided . . . café
on the corner.

1.2

Complete the notes that you started in 1.1. Use the words below to help you.

Note A: brought Ethel with him / gone pick up

Note B: given lift town / be back later

Note C: cut knee / taken hospital

Note D: come join if want to / Jill and Caroline

─── **2** ───────────────────

One possible framework for notes is this:

What has happened	(Roger's just phoned from the station.)
The situation or problem	(He's brought Ethel with him.)
Action	(I've gone to pick them up.)

Work in pairs or small groups. Write notes by filling in the chart below.

	What has happened	*The situation or problem*	*Action*
A		The picture's got stripes on it.	I've taken it back to the shop. Back soon.
B		He's got spots on his face and a high temperature.	
C	Sandra's just phoned. She's in tears.		
D		His wife has walked out on him.	
E			So I've gone over to mend it for him.
F		Bill got jealous, had a row with Sarah, and left the house.	
G	There's been a change of plan.		See you there then?
H		I've passed all my exams!	
I	You'll never guess what's happened!		

─── **3** ───────────────────

Bob and Carol arranged to meet Ted and Alice at the café where they always meet and then go out for the evening. When Ted and Alice did not turn up, Bob and Carol left a note with the waiter.

Write the note again, putting in the words from the column on the right, and the correct punctuation.

ted and alice weve waited for you for half an hour you havent turned up weve decided to go on to the cinema you can come if you like it doesnt start until 7.30 give one of us a ring tomorrow hope you are OK bob and carol 7pm	*WORDS* but or as both still

4

The note in Exercise 3 tells you about a change of plan. Below there are some arrangements. Write change of plan notes. In each case the writer has tried to phone but the other person was out.

A John and Cindy arranged to go out in a foursome with Len and Doris. They arranged to meet at John and Cindy's and go for an Indian meal. But Doris has to work late and they can't go to John and Cindy's at the arranged time. Note from Len or Doris.

B Raymond Williams is having his front room painted. When the painter called to start work Raymond was out. Note from the painter to Raymond Williams.

C You are expecting a friend, Joan, to stay for the weekend. She is due to arrive at six o'clock. But something urgent happens (what?) and you are called away. You will be back soon. Note from you to Joan.

5

The story on the cassette is about some men who are prisoners. It is impossible for them to talk to each other, so they have to plan their escape by passing notes to each other.

Listen to the story on the cassette and write the three notes. The notes start like this: 'We can make clothes (or passports or guns) . . .' Each note is about three sentences long.

5 We are both looking forward to your visit

WRITING LETTERS

CERTAINLY

This unit is designed to give you guided practice in writing letters to English-speaking friends.

─── 1 ───────────────────────────────

Anna is from São Paulo in Brazil. She is coming to Britain next October. Below, there is part of a letter from James Godwin to Anna.

> 24 Bradwell Road
> Oxford OX4 5TP
>
> 27 August 1988
>
> Dear Anna,
> Margaret and I are delighted that you are coming to stay with us. We hope that you enjoy your visit. Maria certainly enjoyed her time with us last year.

> ...and by the way it gets rather cold here in the autumn, so don't forget to bring some warm clothes with you. You'll certainly need a warm coat or an anorak. One more thing, Maria found that a sleeping bag came in useful, because she often slept on friends' floors after parties and so on.
> We are both looking forward to your visit.
> Yours sincerely, James Godwin

1.1

Work in pairs. Which of the statements below about James and Anna are true, which are false and which are uncertain? Write T, F, or U.

1 James does not live alone.
2 Maria came to stay at Bradwell Road.

3 Anna has been to England before.
4 James is a good friend of Anna's.

1.2

Write the phrase in the letter which tells you that the statement is true (T), false (F), or uncertain (U).

2

Claudio, from Italy, is visiting Britain next year. A friend writes to him and tells him what to bring.

2.1

Complete the words under the pictures to make sentences like the example.
Example: You'll need a sleeping bag.

You'll need . . .
Please bring me . . .
Don't forget to bring . . .

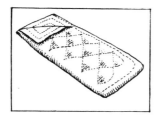

a sleeping bag

an ad........pt........r

warm clothes
a warm coat
an a........

some It............n cheese

tr............'s ch............s

a b............ of It............n
w............

2.2

Work in pairs or small groups. Write as many sentences as you can combining the phrases below with the pictures, like the example.
Example: You'll need a sleeping bag in case you stay with friends overnight.

Phrases

... because we can't get it/them here.
... in case you stay with friends overnight.
... because it's cold here in the autumn.
... you might need it/them.
... because it's one of the Italian specialities that I really like.
... because I know you'll feel the cold when you come over here.
... it's really delicious.
... it's not safe to carry too much cash.
... you'll get a better rate of exchange.

——— 3 ———

An English-speaking friend is coming from another country to stay with you.
You want to give him or her some advice about things that he or she *doesn't* need
to bring.
  Write as many sentences as you can using the phrases below, and adding your
own ideas about what they don't need to bring.
Example: You don't need a visa. It's not necessary.

Phrases

You don't/won't need any/a . . .   . . . you can get that here.
You don't need to bring . . .   . . . it's not necessary.

——— 4 ———

An English-speaking friend is coming from another country to stay with you.

4.1

Work in pairs. Write a list of the different sorts of food you eat in your country.
For example, rice, spaghetti, noodles.

4.2

Work in pairs. Each of you writes down the name of a (different) dish that you eat
in your country. Now describe the dish to the other person. Use the phrases
below.

Phrases

They are / It is a kind of . . .   You eat it with (*something else*)
They are / It is a sort of . . .   It tastes like (*something else*)
You eat it for (*meal*)   It tastes . . .

4.3

You are writing to an English-speaking friend and telling him or her about the
food in your country or region. Write three or four sentences describing a typical
dish.

——— 5 ———

Write a letter to an English-speaking friend who is visiting your country for the
first time. Say that your friend is welcome. Say what your friend should bring and
what he or she does not need to bring. Say that he or she will like the food and
describe some dishes or a typical meal. Say that you are looking forward to seeing
your friend. Use the letter in Exercise 1 to help you.

6 I'm having a party

LETTERS OF INVITATION, ACCEPTANCE AND REFUSAL

In this unit you will look at different kinds of invitations, and practise accepting and declining invitations.

1

Frank Simpson is eighteen. He's a plumber. Alan Wicks is a twenty-year-old university student. Some of the invitations they have received in the last year are shown below.

Work in pairs. What is the relationship between the inviter and Frank or Alan (e.g. friend, parent, colleague, etc.)? Write down the relationship and whether the invitation is formal or informal.

Example: friend, informal

a) Alan, I telephoned but there was no reply. I'm having a party for a few friends before I leave England. I hope you can come. I want to speak to you about a lot of things. Please don't be angry with me. Lots of love, Chantal xx

b) Al, are you still speaking to all your less brilliant mates left behind? No, seriously, we're all really pleased for you. You at Cambridge University (wow!). The old school is having a reunion for us. Your mum's got the official invitation. It's in June when you're on holiday. See you then? If you're coming back to Northampton, of course. All the best, Frank

c)

> PARTY INVITATION
>
> To: Frank Simpson   From: Chantal Deladier
>
> You are invited to a party on: 17th July at: 7:30
>
> At: 21 Longacre Avenue, Northampton.
>
> Please bring a bottle.

d) ... the party was wonderful for me too. Can you come and stay with me in France? It would be marvellous if you could come for Christmas. I know my family would like to meet you. We could go to the Pigalle! Please write soon, Frank. Love, Chantal × ×

e)

HAMFIELDS,

Northampton's leading furniture store, invites you to its

Open Evening.

Many new lines of armchairs, bedroom and garden furniture.

7–9pm Wednesday, 25th July

f)   Just to show we've learned nothing from previous years, we are planning to have another office party this Christmas! Please tick here if you can come ☐. Now the bad news. We'll need to charge £5 a head and ask you to bring a bottle.

—— 2 ——

2.1

With your teacher's help, complete and say these phrases used when accepting or declining invitations. Use invitations that someone made to you or that you know about.

Example: I'd love to come to Catherine's party.

Phrases

	Accepting	*Declining*
Formal	. . . happy to attend . . .	. . . it will not be possible . . . Unfortunately my wife and I have to . . . . . . unable to attend . . .
Informal	. . . love to come . . . . . . looking forward to seeing you there . . .	I'm afraid . . . Unfortunately something else has come up . . . I'd love to but . . . . . . can't make it this time.

19

2.2

Write these invitations using the names of people and places you know. Do not forget to write the time and place. Use Exercise 1 and 2.1 to help you.

a) You want a close friend to go to a disco or nightclub with you. Other friends are coming too.
b) You (or you and your husband/wife/girlfriend/boyfriend) want to invite someone you know fairly well to dinner. You have phoned them several times but they were out each time.
c) You want a friend from an English-speaking country to come and stay with you. Mention some of the things you could do together.
d) You are having a party but you don't want to send out printed party invitations like the one in Exercise 1. Write to a close friend in another town and invite him or her to the party.

—— **3** ——————————————————————————————

Write a letter accepting one of the invitations in 2.2 and a letter declining a different invitation. If you decline an invitation you should give a reason.

7 We're meeting at the restaurant . . .

ARRANGEMENTS IN WRITING

This unit will help you practise making suggestions and arrangements in writing.

———— 1 ——————————————————————

Three friends are coming to stay with you one weekend soon. Where could you take them? What could you do together?

1.1

Work in pairs. Make suggestions and then accept or reject the suggestions, using the phrases below. Use real places that you know and like.

Phrases

Making suggestions	*Accepting*	*Rejecting*
Let's go to . . .	Yes, when?	No, I'm working all this week.
Let's go for . . .	Good idea.	I can't at the moment.
Why don't we meet for . . . ?	What time ?	Tuesday's not possible, Wednesday is.
We're meeting at . . .	Fine.	
Can you meet me . . . ?	Right.	Could we do something else ?
I'll meet you . . .	Sure, what time?	Couldn't we do something else ?
I'll see you at . . .		
I'd like to . . .		

1.2

Some of the suggestions you made in 1.1 were accepted. But the arrangement is with only one of the friends coming for the weekend. Now you want to write to your other friends. Tell them what arrangements have been made.

Write five arrangements that you have made, using 'We + -ing'.
Example: We're meeting at the restaurant at 8 o'clock on Friday and then going on to the cinema.

——— 2 ———

Look at the invitations in Unit 6 Exercise 1 again.

2.1

Here are two telephone conversations between Chantal and Alan and Chantal and Frank. The conversations took place on a hot evening in July.

What do you think is the relationship between Chantal Deladier, Alan Wicks and Frank Simpson?

Telephone conversation 1

Alan: .... Alan.
Chantal: Oh hi, Alan. I was just washing my hair.
Alan: I was wondering .... ?
Chantal: The cinema? Oh Alan, I'm afraid ....
Alan: .... ?
Chantal: Excuse me, Alan, but I think it's my business who I'm going with. You treat me as if I belong to you sometimes. Alan!   Alan!   He's rung off. Stupid boy.

Telephone conversation 2

Chantal: Hello, Frank? Chantal. Frank, ... I want to go somewhere else.
Frank: .... ?
Chantal: Well, I've just realized I've already seen the film.
Frank: .... ?
Chantal: Brights? The nightclub? Yes, that ....
Frank: .... up in fifteen minutes then.
Chantal: Oh, we're going by car? OK, lovely.
Frank: ....
Chantal: Yes, I love you too. Bye-bye, darling.

2.2

Work in pairs. Fill in the missing parts of the conversations.

2.3

Read the complete conversations aloud with your partner.

—— **3** ————————————————————————————

On the cassette you can hear what Alan, Frank and Chantal did that summer in Northampton. There are eleven things altogether.

3.1

Take notes on the eleven things.
Example: Frank – Alan – drink – after school reunion

3.2

Imagine that you are a friend of Frank and Chantal's. You are writing a letter about them to a good friend (or an ex-girlfriend?) of Frank's (gossip!). Write about four of the things that Frank and Chantal did together.
Example: Frank and Chantal went to Brights nightclub. And then they . . .

—— **4** ————————————————————————————

In the end, Frank did not go to Paris to see Chantal, but Alan did. (Why? Any ideas?) The answer is on the cassette.

4.1

Listen to the cassette and take notes. Then write Chantal's letter to Frank, inviting him to Paris and saying what they will do there.

4.2

Write Alan's letter saying that he is coming and asking Chantal to meet him at Paris Nord station. Alan also said he was looking forward to doing various things in Paris with Chantal as his guide. Use your notes from the cassette to help you write the letter.

8 I had a marvellous time . . .

LETTERS OF THANKS

When people do something for you, you often write a letter of thanks. This unit
will give you practice in writing letters of thanks in different situations.

───── **1** ─────────────────────────────────────

You and your family recently stayed with friends in Scotland for a week.

1.1

Work in pairs. Which of these phrases *can't* you use in a letter of thanks?

a) Thank you for putting us up last week.
b) We enjoyed our stay with you.
c) Your house is quite nice.
d) Thank you for the bed and the food.
e) It was lovely to see you all last week.
f) We will recommend your house to other people.
g) We will always remember the trip to Edinburgh.
h) The weekend with you was nice, but our visits to Scotland are always nice.
i) The meal in that restaurant in Edinburgh was all right.
j) It was interesting to meet Bob and Tina.
k) Your house is much nicer than Bob and Tina's.
l) You must come and stay with us soon.
m) Your children are nice.
n) Wasn't the scenery on the west coast fantastic!

1.2

Work in pairs. With your teacher's help, rewrite the phrases above that you can't
use in a letter of thanks. (The phrases that you can use may help you to do this.)

2

Work in pairs. Match the thanking phrases on the left with the situations on the
right.

Thanking phrases

 1 I had a marvellous time.
 2 I appreciated your help the other night.
 3 It goes really well with my trousers.
 4 It was good of you to help us out with
    James.
 5 We always enjoy your company.
 6 You shouldn't have!
 7 I hope he was no trouble.
 8 I hope I didn't put you to too much trouble.
 9 It made my day!
10 The food was superb.

Situations

   Someone . . .
A has given you a birthday present.
B gave an enjoyable party.
C put you up for the night.
D looked after your small child when you
   were away.

3

Work in pairs. Write as many phrases as you can to thank someone for:
a) Lending you something (What did they lend you? For how long?).
b) A present you didn't expect (What was the present? Why did they give it to you?).
c) A surprise (What was the surprise?).
d) Helping you to do something difficult (What?).

4

Read this thank you letter from Anne to Tim, who lives in Germany. Work in
pairs. Take out the underlined phrases and write the letter again using some of
the phrases listed below instead.

Dear Tim,
    Just a line to say thank you for the food you sent
from Germany. It was very thoughtful of you to choose
things that we can't get easily here. I'm using the dried
mushrooms for cooking and we've started on the German
biscuits already!
    John and Louise send their love.
                              Love,
                              Anne

Phrases

a) This is just . . .
b) ever so kind . . .
c) begun to eat . . .
d) This is my letter . . .
e) had to start . . .
f) thanks a lot . . .
g) really annoying . . .
h) I'm writing . . .
i) I can always use . . .
j) a good idea . . .
k) I'm cooking with . . .
l) many thanks . . .

—— **5** ——————————————————————————

5.1

Work in pairs. One of you reads A, and the other reads B. Then describe the presents.

> **A** You don't live in Britain. You live in (*your country*). You are visiting B. B is an old friend and he or she lives in Britain. Write down three presents that you can bring B from your country. The presents must be things that B can't get easily in Britain. Tell B why you like these three things and (if necessary) tell B what to do with them or how to use them. You start the discussion when B is ready.

> **B** You live in Britain. Your friend A came to stay with you and brought three very nice presents. When A is ready to go back home, you buy three presents for A. The presents are all things that you can get more easily in Britain than in A's country. Try to think of three typically British presents and write them down. Then tell A why you like these three things and (if necessary) tell A what to do with them or how to use them. A will start the discussion when you are ready.

5.2

Read A's and B's roles again. A has now gone home to his or her country. A and B write to each other and say what they are doing with the presents and how they are using them.

Write a letter as A or B. Use the framework below to help you and use the letter in Exercise 4 as a model (it has the same framework).

Framework

1 Opening (e.g. Dear Tim).
2 Why you are writing (e.g. Just a line . . .).
3 Thanks and details (what you are doing with the present).
4 Concluding the letter.
5 Closing (Love, Best wishes, All the best, Yours).
6 Signature.

—— **6** ——————————————————————

Listen to the conversations on the cassette, then write these thank you letters.

Letter 1: Julie to John and Jim

Letter 2: Klaus to Alexander

SECTION 3: OFFICIAL WRITING — FORMS, MEMOS AND LETTERS

9 What is the starting salary?

FILLING IN OFFICIAL FORMS

In this unit you will practise filling in official forms in different situations.

─── 1 ───

Ian Stewart started his own computer company two years ago. It has been very successful. Last week Ian saw an advertisement for the East Anglian Prisoners Scheme (E.A.P.S.) in a local newspaper. E.A.P.S. helps prisoners in the East of England find jobs when they leave prison. Ian and another company wrote letters replying to the advertisement.

   Read the two letters and then fill in the Employer's Questionnaire that E.A.P.S. sent them.

Letter 1

Computerama

153 STRAIGHT ROAD   IPSWICH IP4 3RN   Tel (0473) 549260

27 June 1988

Dear Sir,
        I am writing in reply to your advertisement in the East Anglian Gazette, 18 June. We are a small Company, at present. I am the Company Director and there are ten people under me. But that means that anybody starting with us now could have a top job in a few years' time. Your scheme is new to me and I must tell you that I couldn't take anyone convicted of murder or another serious crime. But a young person who just made a mistake could do well with us right now. We start our salespeople on £14,000 p.a. after training.
   Please let me know if this is of interest to you.

        Yours faithfully,
        Ian Stewart
        Ian Stewart

Letter 2

Lesley Downes
Chief Executive

27 June 1988.

Kleenbrite

64 Reynard Street, Lowestoft LO9 5PQ
Tel: (0502) 845161

Dear John,

Sheila Tovey is doing very well, you'll be pleased to hear! We could use another girl, if you have one. Same job, office cleaning, but the pay is £5 an hour (the best in the area!)

Anyone will do, as long as they work hard and are happy cleaning offices, as that's all we've got!

Excuse the scribble, must rush, the phone is ringing.

All the best,
Lesley.

East Anglian Prisoners Scheme: Employer's Questionnaire

1   Name: ....

2   Name of company: ....

3   Address and telephone no. of company: ....

3   Your position in the company: ....

5   Have you participated in the scheme before? ....

6   If so, who did you employ? ....

7   What position would the E.A.P.S. client hold? ....

8   Is the position permanent? ....

9   Is the position full-time? ....

10   What is the starting salary? ....

11   Are there promotion possibilities? ....

....

12   Are there any circumstances in which an E.A.P.S. member would not be acceptable? ....

....

───── **2** ───

John Fredericks of the E.A.P.S. found someone for both of the companies. Their photographs are below.

Neil Jackson

Julie Gable

Work in pairs or groups. With your teacher's help, fill in the Client's Questionnaire for each of them.

East Anglian Prisoners Scheme: Client's Questionnaire

1 Name: ....

2 Address: ....

3 Tel: ....

4 Education: ....

5 Previous Employment: ....

6 Any other skills (e.g. languages, typing, carpentry): ....

7 Crime: ....

8 Length of prison sentence: ....

Brief personal assessment based on E.A.P.S. interview.   **CONFIDENTIAL**

....

....

....

....

....

——— 3 ———

You work for a company. Recently you went on a trip abroad on company business for the weekend (Friday night to Monday morning).

Decide what your job is in the company and why you went on this trip. For example, you could be a journalist after a story, you could be a Sales Executive trying to sell abroad (sell what, where and to whom?).

The boss is a friend of yours and you know she does not check expenses very carefully. So you spent a lot of money. When you got back you found you had a new boss. This one is trying to cut down on staff expenses.

3.1

Fill in the Staff Expenses Form honestly. (Remember you spent too much money.)

Staff Expenses Form

1 Name: ....

2 Position in the company: ....

3 Purpose of visit: ....

4 Length of visit: ....

5 Expenses breakdown·

		£	p
a) Name of hotel			
b) Hotel bills (amount in £ or US $)			
c) Extras at the hotel (newspapers, telephone calls, etc.): .... Please itemize.			
d) Meals and drinks (entertainment): please state the name of the person with you, the purpose of the entertainment and the outcome of the meeting.			
e) Other entertainment (nightclubs, etc.): fill in as for (d).			
f) Travel expenses: please itemize and produce receipts, tickets, etc.			

3.2

Work in pairs. Give your Staff Expenses Form to the person next to you. One of you is the new boss, trying to cut down expenses. The other is the member of staff who filled in the expenses form. The boss criticizes the staff member's expenses. The member of staff tries to justify them. Have a discussion. Use the phrases below to help you.

Phrases

Boss	*Staff member*
How can you justify . . . ?	It was necessary/essential to . . .
How did you manage to spend . . . ?	But look what the company got out of it. We . . .
Why did you spend . . . ?	The cost of living in . . .
Couldn't you have stayed . . . ?	I needed to . . .

10 Anyone who wishes to come into the building over the weekend

WRITING MEMOS

A memo is a short message written by one person to another in the same business organization. In this unit you will look at how memos are written, before practising writing your own.

1

Nikola Weishaupt (who is German) works for CCC, a multinational company. CCC uses English in all its branches. Here are two memos that she wrote. She later improved one of them.

1.1

Which memo needs to be improved?

Memo A

> *From:* NW   *To:* Marketing Department
>
> As you know there have, unfortunately, been several burglaries in the building recently. For this reason, from next Monday, only Mrs Leclerc, Mr Akimura and myself will keep keys to the front door. Anyone who wishes to come into the building over the weekend or after 9 pm on a weekday, please ask one of these people for a key.

Memo B

> *From:* NW   *To:* Marketing Department
>
> If you want to use the photocopier, go to Room 342 from now on. Mrs Clarke will make any copies you need. We are losing too many copies and the machine keeps breaking down. Sign the Photocopying Book and say which department you are from and the purpose of the copies.

1.2

Rewrite the memo which needs to be improved, using the good memo to help you.

2

Write memos in these situations. Discuss what you will put into your memo with the person next to you before you start. Use the phrases below each situation to help you.

Situation A

People in the marketing department have been complaining that their colleagues are smoking too much. The office is open-plan and some non-smokers cannot get on with their work. Following these complaints Nikola Weishaupt decided to send a memo asking people not to smoke in the office.

Phrases

Following complaints that . . .   Please bear in mind that . . .   non-smokers are finding that . . .   in the interests of the efficiency of the department . . .   I must ask you . . .   would you mind refraining from . . .   please cooperate by . . .

Situation B

One year later the office changed from open-plan to individual offices. Nikola Weishaupt sent everyone a copy of the diagram below and also sent a brief memo. She said who was sharing with whom and who the new secretary or PA (personal assistant) was. She said she hoped the new arrangement was agreeable to everybody.

Phrases

With reference to the attached . . .   please see the diagram . . .   from now on . . .   his or her new PA is . . .   I very much hope that . . .   if there are any problems with these arrangements . . .

MARKETING DEPARTMENT

Marketing Manager	Assistant Marketing Managers	Sales Team
Nikola Weishaupt	Marie-Louise Leclerc	Adriana Rossi
PA: Claude Tanvier	Toshi Akimura	Abdullah al-Bin Ali
	PA: George French	Erik Halgren
		Anamick Grounwoud
		Secretary: Barbara Manegold
Typing pool	Photocopies and stationery Mrs Clarke	Other departments

—— **3** ————————————————————————————

3.1

Look at the diagram of the CCC Marketing Department in Exercise 2 again. The Sales Team are all young and in most cases this is their first job after school or college. The secretary is eighteen. The Assistant Marketing Managers are in their early thirties. Imagine that you are one of the people in the diagram (but not Nikola Weishaupt).

Work in groups of three or four. Choose who you are from the diagram (make sure everyone in the group is someone different from the diagram).

Choose some of the grievances from the list below. Think about what the grievances have meant to *you personally* and make notes that you can use later at a Marketing Department meeting.

Grievances

A It is not possible to smoke in the office any more. 'No Smoking' signs were put up but there was no consultation with the staff first.
B You now have to share an office with someone who smokes (who?). It is making you ill.
C Before the change the Marketing Manager and her two assistants had one PA. They now have two and the Sales Team has lost one of its secretaries.
D The old open-plan was much better than the cramped and poky individual offices.
E The coffee machine is now in Ms Weishaupt's office. When the office was open-plan everybody could use it.
F There is now no direct access to the photocopier or stationery. Everything has to go through Mrs Clarke.
G This is confidential. There is someone, now in the same office as you, who you just cannot work with. It's a personality clash. You just can't stand him or her.

Role play   In your groups role play the CCC Marketing Department meeting. Say how *you* feel about your grievances. One of the group is Group Secretary and should take notes on the discussion and report back to the class as a whole when the discussion is finished.

3.2

Write a memo to Nikola Weishaupt about your grievances. Write on your own or with the group. Use the phrases below to help you.

Phrases

I would like to point out . . .   I would respectfully suggest . . .   this controversial decision . . .   the unfortunate lack of consultation . . .   has created problems in the office . . .   this has meant . . .   I am disappointed that . . .   is a threat to the smooth running of the department . . .

11 I am applying for the post of . . .

WRITING CVs, REPLYING TO JOB AND OTHER ADVERTISEMENTS

In this unit you will look at different sorts of advertisements and practise writing a CV about yourself, a letter of application and replies to different advertisements. (CV stands for Curriculum Vitae. It is a brief account of your career.)

--- **1** ---

Below, there is a job advertisement from *The Guardian* on 29 July. Teresa Price applied for the job. You can see her CV and part of her letter of application below.

1.1

Complete the letter of application using information from the advertisement and the CV to help you.

A GERMAN ADVERTISING AGENCY

with an international clientele is looking for a 24 to 30-year-old graduate in British Economics. The ability to work under pressure together with an enthusiasm to learn and good command of German is essential since you would be based in Germany except for brief trips to the London office.

Please send a letter of application and c.v. to: 24 Tottenham Street, London W1.

```
          C V
TERESA PRICE

Born: 1960, Grantham, Lincolnshire
Education:
1971–7: Grantham Comprehensive (9 0 levels, A level
  Economics, French, German)
1977–80: Bristol University, BSc Economics (2nd class
  honours)
Employment:
1980–4: Social Worker, East Anglian Prisoners Scheme
1984–Present: Advertising Copywriter, Marksad, Norwich
Marital status: Single
Hobbies: Travel, music
Referees: John Fredericks, E.A.P.S. (Director)
          Arthur Cuttler, Marksad (Director)
```

⫸→

```
Dear Sir,
        In answer to your ..... I am applying for the
post of advertising executive.
        I have a background in economics. I ..... at
Bristol University and obtained ..... (please see
attached CV). I also have a good ..... German, as you
mention in your advertisement.
        I am interested in the job because .....
        I would be happy to attend for interview if
selected.
        Yours .....,


        Teresa Price
```

1.2

Choose a job that you would like to do (either a full-time job or a summer job). Write out your CV using Teresa's CV to help you.

Write a letter of application for the job in answer to an advertisement for it in a newspaper. Use Teresa's letter to help you.

—— 2 ——

Here are some different types of newspaper advertisements.

2.1

Find an advertisement offering rented holiday accommodation, a holiday exchange advertisement, and two lonely hearts advertisements below.

A **Company Director.**
Widower seeks attractive lady companion, age 30–40 for outings, holidays and friendship.
Box No. C42

B **CHEST** Freezer v.g.c. £50.
Two Classical Guitars with cases £15 each.
.25ct Diamond Solitaire size M ring (not worn) £150 o.n.o.

C
Do you have a real problem?
Then let me help. I am a genuine clairvoyant and psychic counsellor with many years experience. Only sincere enquiries please.

D **Staff Nurse,** 26, slim, attractive, non-smoker. Interests: music, tennis, films. Seeks gentleman 20–30 with similar interests.
Box No. M523

E

Carpenter's Cottages
Delightful holiday cottages
in Holt, Norfolk, close to
coast. Each cottage sleeps
4–6. Colour TV. Pets and
children welcome. Meter
electricity.
Edward Wilson, Holt

F   **3 bedroom** semi-detached
chalet bungalow. Lounge/
diner, kitchen, bathroom,
double-glazed, wall insu-
lation, air conditioning,
central heating, garage,
garden with fruit trees
and patio area.
£69,500 Freehold

H   **Offer** 3 bedroom house, nice
dining room/lounge in
beautiful Yorkshire dales.
One month this summer.
Anywhere attractive con-
sidered for holiday
exchange.
Arnold Sidebottom,
Hawes, Yorkshire.

G   **DOG CLIPPING** Also groom-
ing and bathing. Have your
dog prepared for the summer
sun. Phone Wendy (Any
time).

2.2

Write a letter in answer to advertisement E in 2.1 above. Sometimes more than
one of the choices below is correct.

a) *Dear Sir,*
b) *Dear Edward Wilson,*
c) *Dear Mr Wilson,*

a) *In reply to your advertisement*
b) *I saw your advertisement in today's newspaper and*
c) *You advertised in today's newspaper*

a) *I am interested in a holiday at Carpenter's cottages.*
b) *I want to come to Carpenter's cottages.*
c) *I like Carpenter's cottages.*

a) *some information about the cottages*
Please send me b) *your brochure*
c) *further details*

a) *the cost*
including b) *the price*   *for a family of five including two children for a*
c) *the amount*

a) *Is there a price reduction*
fortnight. b) *Is it cheaper*   *for children under the age of five?*
c) *Do we pay less*

a) *Yours faithfully,*
b) *Yours sincerely,*
c) *With best wishes,*

Mercedes Sanchez
Barcelona, Spain

——— 3 —————————————————————————————

Reply to advertisement H in 2.1. Write about your home and family. Use the framework below to help you.

Greeting
Enquiry about exchange
Description of your home
Description of the area
Who is in your family
The date of the exchange
You hope for a reply (I look forward . . .)
Closing (Yours . . .)
Signature

——— 4 —————————————————————————————

Read advertisement D in 2.1 again. Here is a reply to the Staff Nurse's advertisement but there are no capital letters, commas, apostrophes or full stops. Put in all the punctuation. There are four paragraphs in the letter.

```
                              Richard Meadows
                              14A Gillon Street
                              Bristol BS5 9E4
                              Tel. 351294

                              17 March 1988

   dear madam i read your advertisement in todays daily
   globe with great interest im 22 and a student in my
   first year at bristol university studying medicine so we
   should have something in common im interested in music
   too though you didnt say what kind of music you like
   personally i like classical music and some jazz i also
   go to films whenever i can im afraid i dont like tennis
   or any other sport much but i go walking in leigh woods a
   lot would that interest you i know people think a
   students life is full of parties and fun and girls but
   since i came to bristol six months ago i have found that
   its difficult to really make friends here so could we
   perhaps meet and have a meal together some time please
   give me a ring with best wishes richard ps ive got a car
   do you fancy a drive at the weekend
```

——— 5 🖭 —————————————————————————————

On the cassette you can hear four people on a 'lonely hearts' radio programme. Choose one of them and write to him or her. Use the letter in Exercise 4 to help you. Take notes from the cassette as you listen.

12 I was most dissatisfied. . .

LETTERS OF COMPLAINT

In this unit you will think about different situations you might want to complain about. You will look at how letters of complaint are written, and then write your own.

─── **1** ───────────────────────────────

1.1

Work in pairs. Complain to the person next to you about a product or a service. Use the phrases below to help you, and use the pictures to give you ideas.
Example: I was most dissatisfied with the coat. It tore when I put it on.

Phrases

. . . most dissatisfied with . . .
. . . was not satisfactory. . .

. . . I wish/want to complain about . . .

I was disappointed with . . .
. . . was simply not good
  enough . . .

1.2

Tom Lake has just come back from his holiday. He was so angry about the holiday that he wrote notes all over the holiday brochure. Later he wrote to Awayholidays and complained. He also asked for a refund (his money back) so his letter started like this:

> Dear Sir,
>   I wish to complain about my Awayholiday to Amsterdam.

and his letter ended like this:

> I think you should refund all the money I paid for this holiday. I look forward to hearing from you.
> Yours faithfully,
> Tom Lake.

Read the brochure and Tom's notes and write the letter. Use the phrases from 1.1 to help you.

AWAYHOLIDAYS:

The Holidays of a Lifetime. — Ha – ha – ha

We take the night ferry at Harwich and arrive at the Hook of Holland in time for breakfast. — Not in time for lunch

Ferry on strike

From the Hook we go to lovely Amsterdam and have lunch in the heart of the city.

Then we go to our hotel, the three-star Frans Hals in the centre of the city. This is one of the best hotels in Amsterdam. — True, but it was full. Stayed in one-star hotel, breakfast poor, service worse. Awful!

On our first day we visit the Rijksmuseum and Anne Frank's house. — No time

Great! The only thing I enjoyed

On our second day there is a trip by boat round the famous canals. The afternoon of the second day is free for shopping.

On our third day we go to the Isle of Marken, the famous island where the Dutch still wear their national costume. — Yes! And had to pay extra for it. It doesn't say that here, does it?

On the fourth day we tra...

─── **2** ───

Have a look at 'Making your complaint' from the leaflet 'How to Put Things Right' published by the Office of Fair Trading.

Making your complaint

To make a complaint:

* stop using the item
* tell the shop at once
* take it back (if you can)
* take a receipt or proof of purchase (if you can)
* ask for the manager or owner
* keep calm!

If it is a tricky problem it may be better to write. To be on the safe side you could use recorded delivery. Keep copies of all letters. Do not send receipts or other proof of purchase — give reference numbers or send photocopies. If you have a guarantee see **Guarantees,** over the page.

If you phone:

* first, make a note of what you want to say
* have receipts and useful facts handy
* get the name of the person you speak to
* jot down the date and time and what is said
* keep calm!

If the local shop or office cannot help, contact the managing director at the head office. Find out if the firm belongs to a trade association. Some associations will intervene in disputes. Those with Codes of Practice have a special system for dealing with complaints.

If you see a notice like this you can do two things:

1 Ignore it. 2 Tell your Trading Standards Department. Such notices are illegal, even for sale goods.
A trader *cannot* wriggle out of his responsibility if he sells you faulty goods.

Now complete this chart in writing.

Yesterday I bought . . .

	What?	*Receipt or guarantee?*	*From where?*	*When I . . .*	*What happened?*
a)	a can of beans	no	my supermarket	opened it	I found a nail in it
b)	a TV	both		got it home	
c)		no	my butcher's shop	unwrapped it	it . . .
d)		receipt			it wouldn't write
e)		both		got it home	there was/were no . . .
f)		receipt			it wouldn't record
g)		both			one of the wheels fell off

—— **3** ————————————————————

3.1

In which of these situations would you write a letter of complaint?

a) You bought a jacket or a skirt on holiday in America. When you got it home the lining fell out.

b) Your train or bus to work is late every day.

c) You were on holiday in Australia last month. Your train to the airport was two hours late and you missed the plane home.

d) Your next door neighbour had a noisy party last night. This is the first time this has happened.

e) A man in your office or factory smokes all the time. You don't smoke and you don't like it. You have asked him to stop smoking. He hasn't.

f) A furniture shop has telephoned you five times this week with invitations to go to their Sale Week. They sometimes phone late and have got you out of bed twice.

g) Some hi-fi equipment was delivered yesterday. You have just noticed that the bill is for £500. The equipment is listed in the catalogue at £350. When you telephoned, a man said, 'Sorry I can't help you. There's nothing I can do.'

3.2

Work in small groups. Choose one of the situations from 3.1 where you would write a letter of complaint.
    Discuss the situation with the group and note some phrases for complaining.
    Write the letter together. Use this framework from Exercise 2 to help you.

What?
Receipt or guarantee?
From where?
When I . . .
What happened?

4

You are complaining about something and you hope it will improve in the future. Here are some phrases to say that. The phrases come at the end of letters of complaint.

Phrases

I hope that from now on you will
    stop . . .
Perhaps next time you will think
    about . . .

In future, would you please . . .
I hope this won't happen again.

Listen to two conversations on the cassette and use the framework below to write two letters of complaint. Use the phrases above for the 'improve in the future' paragraph.

Framework
Writing to complain
Problem
Improve in the future

Letter 1: Write to the couple in the flat above.
Letter 2: Write to the parents of the three boys.

—— **5** ————————————————————————————

Think of something that has made you angry recently, something you could write a letter of complaint about. Use Exercise 3 to give you ideas.

Make notes about the situation.

Using your notes, tell your teacher and the class what happened.

Write a letter of complaint about the situation.

SECTION 4: EXTENSIVE WRITING —
PEOPLE, PLACES AND EVENTS

13 He's overweight, she's quite slim
DESCRIBING APPEARANCE

In this unit you will look at people's appearance, including their faces, height, build and clothes. You will then practise writing descriptions.

——— **1** ———————————————————————————

1.1

Work in pairs. Below, there are descriptions of people. One of them is from a letter. Where are the others from? Use a dictionary if you don't know a word in English.

a) Loren, Sophia b. 20 Sept. 1934 Italy. Actress m. Carlo Ponti. Made first film appearance as extra in 'Quo Vadis', has appeared in num. films inclng 'El Cid' 1963, 'Hot Autumn' 1970.

b) Her name's Chantal. This is a bit embarrassing actually, because she's only seventeen and still at school. I'll be accused of baby snatching! No, I think the main thing was that I felt totally relaxed with her. We just . . .

c) I was born . . . a subject of Francis Joseph who acceded to the throne in 1848. The Kaiser ruled Germany, Bulgaria had a Czar, the last Sultan of Turkey had recently been dethroned and radio – let alone television – was not yet invented. I am older than the BBC . . .

d) Her hands were strong, capable as her spare middle-aged face. She was a handsome woman; she had never been beautiful or even pretty. Her skin was marked by the sun, harshened and there were wrinkles around her eyes as she peered into the sun-blazing highway. Her name was Belinda, and she was going home.

e) Marx worked prodigiously, spending full days from 10 am to 7 pm in the library of the British Museum, studying both old and new books on economics. However, he did not stick to this task continually . . . It is possible that Marx became bored at times with the study of economics.

1.2

With your teacher's help write a short description of someone you know or someone famous in the style of *one* of these descriptions. Say where your description would be from, for example, from a letter, a biography, a novel. Write accordingly.

—— **2** ——

Work in groups. Look at these photographs and react to them. Say everything you can about the people in them, using the phrases to give you ideas. Imagine that you met one of these people on holiday. Write a short description of the person as part of a letter to a friend.

Phrases

He/she looks like a . . .   He/she seems . . .
He/she looks . . .   I like/don't like him/her because . . .
He/she has . . .   I think he's/she's . . .
He/she's got . . .

—— **3** ——

3.1

Work in pairs. Look at these drawings. Which of the phrases below can you use to describe the drawings?
hook nose, wavy hair, pointed chin, chubby cheeks, curly hair, brunette, lovely eyes, full lips, balding, a round face, spots, a moustache and beard, thick glasses, blonde hair, wrinkles, handsome, beautiful, thin lips, granny glasses

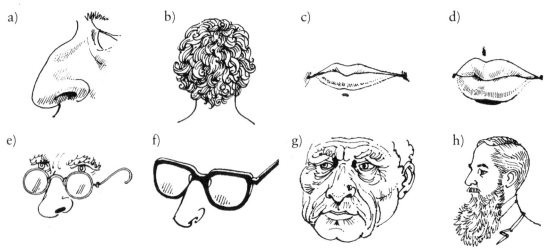

a)   b)   c)   d)

e)   f)   g)   h)

3.2

Which of the phrases in 3.1 would please you if someone said them about you?

──── **4** ──

Below there are four categories for the phrases in Exercise 3. Write more words
or phrases for each category.

Categories

| Noses | Type and colour of hair (including moustaches and beards) | Complexion | Evaluation (e.g. handsome) |

Think of someone you know, either someone in your family, a friend, or a well-
known person. Describe that person's face, in three or four sentences.

──── **5** ──

5.1

Match the descriptions below to the drawings, where possible. Some descriptions
have no drawing.

Descriptions

a)  b)  c)

Height
taller than average
a little man
medium height
a bit shorter than I am

Build
she's quite slim
she's a bit plump
a broad-shouldered man
well-built
stocky
a thin man
he's overweight

d)  e)  f)

5.2

Which of the phrases in 5.1 would please you if someone said them about you?
Compare your answer with the person next to you.
　　Look at the phrases that would *not* please you. Can you change them to make
them more complimentary?

──── **6** ────────────────────────────────────

Work in pairs. Look at these sentences:
She was wearing a | nice, light blue, cotton | dress.
　　　　She had a | nice, light blue, cotton | dress on.

Add as many words as you can to the chart below. Here are a few words to give
you some ideas: pale green, leather, anorak, fashionable, shoes, tight-fitting.

Judgement	*Colour*	*Material*	*Type of clothes*
nice	light blue	cotton	dress

──── **7** ────────────────────────────────────

Write two or three paragraphs describing someone in your family or a friend.
Describe his or her appearance and clothes and write your opinion of him or her.
OR do the same, describing a famous person. Again, imagine that you are writing
a letter to a friend about the person. If you are describing a famous person
imagine that you have just met him or her (where? how?).

14 He's getting married soon

DESCRIBING PEOPLE, THEIR JOBS AND THEIR LIVES

This unit will give you the opportunity to think about different jobs that people do, and then practise writing descriptions of people and their lives.

—— **1** ————————————————————————————

1.1

Look at the occupations below. In groups, choose three of the lists and decide whether each job is skilled or unskilled.

sailor	mechanic	zoo keeper
doctor	plumber	police officer
footballer	politician	film star
labourer	hotel receptionist	courier
probation officer	journalist	bricklayer
bus driver	farmer	model
waiter/waitress	pilot	writer
lawyer	tennis player	carpenter
athlete	train driver	engineer
gardener	factory worker	artist
musician	vet	businessman/woman
nurse	typist	electrician
shop assistant	soldier	traffic warden
teacher	student	judge

Now sort them out under these headings. Some jobs will go into several categories.

manual   professional   outdoor   office-based   involving travel involving danger

1.2

In pairs or groups choose one occupation and note down three good points and three bad points about the job.

1.3

Now imagine the person doing the job you have chosen. Write about the person using the description below as a model.

Description

Robin is a probation officer. He and his wife are friends of ours. As a senior probation officer he sees people who have come out of prison and are on probation, and he has just written a report on a man called Jeremy Bamber. Bamber was convicted of murder recently and the judge considered Robin's report when he sentenced Bamber.

Probation officers are not very well paid. Robin gets about £15,000 a year, I think. He works very hard and often doesn't get home until eight or nine in the evening.

He spends most of his spare time with his wife and two young sons, and at the weekends he grows vegetables in his garden. He is a quiet, reserved man who doesn't say much and prefers listening to talking. Perhaps that comes from his job.

2

Imagine that the person you wrote about in Exercise 1 wants to change his or her job. Write a paragraph saying why, and what is better about the new job. Here are some phrases to give you some ideas:

Phrases

He quite likes the job but . . .   she doesn't get enough . . .   more interesting . . .   he's getting married soon and . . .   she's an outgoing, lively person and . . .   the job doesn't suit him because . . .   more of a challenge . . .

---

3 🖭

Here are some of the words and phrases on the cassette. Go through them, then write descriptions of two of the people on the cassette.

Phrases

works too hard, conscientious, well paid, fairly pretty, gorgeous, a midget, a successful air about him, unreliable, breath smells, a stunning figure, terrifically efficient, dynamic and energetic, a self-made man, a millionaire, has got good taste, distinguished, modest

—— **4** ————————————————————————————————

4.1

Work in groups. Make notes about yourself in ten years' time. Using your notes to help you, give a talk to your group about yourself in ten years' time.

4.2

Write about yourself in ten years' time. Write three or four paragraphs (about one page).

15 Mountains, jungles, deserts, lakes and tropical beaches

DESCRIBING PLACES

In this unit you will look at various descriptions of places before practising
writing your own descriptions of places you know.

───── **1** ──

Below there are pictures of six places and a brief description of them.

1.1

Match
the places
and the
descriptions.

a)

d)

b)

e)

c)

f)

1 Stockholm. A view of the old town. The old city was built on the island of Staden in the channel linking Lake Mälar with the Baltic. The picturesque cluster of houses reach right down to the water.

2 Marseilles. The old harbour overlooked by the church of Notre Dame de la Garde.

3 The wonderfully busy streets of Penang, where the foot and the pedal still rule the road. Fish, fruit, bread, machinery, people, everything rolls on the bicycle wheel beneath fluttering laundry and garish signs.

4 Lake Caláfquen, southern Chile. A peaceful place where time stands still and the only sound is the lapping of the water.

5 The streets in the old city of Tallinn, capital of Estonia. While the days are very short in winter, in summer they stretch well into the nights, especially in June, when you can see the famous 'White Nights'.

6 Mexico City. We see the imposing National Palace. And for the lover of natural beauty Mexico offers an unequalled variety of scenery – mountains, jungles, deserts, lakes and tropical beaches.

1.2

Work in pairs. Discuss the six places and put them in order of preference from one to six (one is the place you would most like to visit, six the place you would least like to visit). You and your partner must agree.

Join pairs to make groups of four. The two pairs must agree on an order of preference from one to six.

1.3

You work for the Tourist Board in your region. You want to attract more tourists to your region because it has so much to offer.

Choose a town, village, beauty spot or area that you know about in your country.

Describe what the town, village, beauty spot or area looks like. Write one or two paragraphs, using the phrases below to help you. You can use and refer to photographs and pictures of your tourist area if you want to.

Phrases

Places of interest include . . .
The . . . dates from the . . . century . . .
The houses were built of . . .
in . . .

There is the . . . Church/Cathedral/Museum.
. . . beautiful, unspoilt sandy beaches . . .
. . . lovely woods and countryside . . .
. . . beautiful scenery . . .

2

Group discussions. Work with your teacher and the rest of your group.

2.1

Describe and discuss local traditions in your country or your area. For example, a tourist visiting Britain may be interested in the Boat Race in early April or the Christmas traditions at the end of the year. To take another example, is there a Carnival in your country in February? If so, what happens?

2.2

Describe and discuss local industries or crafts that would interest a visitor. For example, if you live in Amsterdam you would take a visitor to a diamond cutter; and many countries have leather or perfume factories open to the public. Which industries or crafts would you show a visitor from abroad and what would the visitor see?

2.3

Discuss the politeness customs in your area. For example, in some countries it is best to say 'May I join you?' before you sit down with strangers in a pub or a bar. And in Britain you always say 'please' and 'thank you' even when you order a meal. To take other examples, do you shake hands in your country? If so, when and who do you shake hands with? And are there different politeness customs for men and for women?

2.4

Write three or four paragraphs giving information about your area to visitors from abroad. Use this framework:
(from 2.1) Traditions (throughout the year)
(from 2.2) Industries and crafts (for visitors)
(from 2.3) Politeness customs
Remember, you want to attract tourists to your area.

3

Ursula Kramer, from Austria, visited friends in Colchester. Her friends used the leaflet 'How to get the best from two days in and around Colchester' to plan Ursula's itinerary. Ursula later wrote a letter to a friend describing the itinerary.

How to get the best from two days in and around

Colchester

England's oldest recorded town

Day 1

Morning: Visit Colchester's famous zoo at Stanway (2 miles)
OR
Take a trip around Dedham Vale, the country of John Constable, Stoke-by-Nayland, Flatford, East Bergholt, Dedham (visit the Heavy Horse Centre there). Quiet villages with half timbered houses. Large churches linked by leafy country lanes.

Afternoon: Visit Colchester itself, England's oldest recorded town. See the Castle and Museum (Roman and British antiquities). Holly Tree Museum (18th and 19th Century objects). Natural History Museum, The Folk Museum, St. John's Abbey (15th Century Gate House), St. Botolph's Priory (part Norman), the Roman Walls and much else. Guided tours from Tourist Information Centre.

Evening: Try the Restaurants on North Hill, William Scraggs, (sea food) or Bistro 9 (French and English home cooking) or try The Albert, North Hill roundabout (Berni Inn) or take a stroll (10 minutes) and enjoy the hospitality of The Sun (probably suits younger people better) or The Crown (Beer Garden)

All Day

Lie on the beach and enjoy the seaside at Clacton (a cheerful, friendly resort – plenty to do and see on wet days), or Frinton (more restrained)
OR
Take a trip to the famous Tiptree strawberry fields (pick your own in season) and on to Maldon (old buildings, Thames Barges). Return home via Goldhanger, Tolleshunt D'Arcy and Mersea Oyster Fishery at East Mersea open 1st Friday in each month or by arrangement.
OR
Take a trip to rural Suffolk, Sudbury (birth place of Gainsborough), Long Melford, Bury St. Edmunds, Lavenham.

Evening: Try the Red Lion in the High Street or treat yourself at le Talbooth (Dedham).

Plus

Trips to Cambridge (1 ½ hours)
London (50 minutes by train) County Cricket (Chelmsford or Colchester) Association Football (Ipswich and Colchester) Mercury Theatre
Cinemas and Nightclubs
Fishing
Golf
Horse Riding
Sports Centre

Day 2

Morning: Visit Fingringhoe Nature Reserve and Nature Trail (Closed Mondays – Ask at Reception for opening hours)
OR
Visit the Antique Shops of Coggeshall (10 miles) over 100 scheduled historic buildings.

Afternoon: Visit Beth Chatto's Garden of unusual plants at Elmstead Market (5 miles). (Closed Sundays and Bank Holidays)
OR
Visit Stour Valley Railway Centre – old engines & special Steam days.

3.1

Read the leaflet and Ursula's letter. There is one mistake in every line of the letter.
Rewrite the letter, correcting the mistakes, in less than ten minutes.

1   dear Gill,
2   We've been having a fairly lovely time here.
3   On Monday we went in the zoo which is a
4   very large one with a sea in the middle. It
5   also bred the first Zedonk of the world. A
6   Zedonk, apparently, is cross between a zebra
7   and donkey.
8   Later on we went over Colchester,
9   where you can still see part off the old
10 roman wall. We also visited St John's Abbey,
11 which is fiveteenth century. In the evening,
12 when the children have gone to bed,
13 we tried Colchester oysters, a local specialism,
14 by Scraggs sea food restaurant.
15   Next day we go to a village called
16 Fingringhoe, a couple of miles from Colchester, what
17 has a Nature Reserve. I did bird watching
18 there for the first time in our life. Then Len
19 drove us to Coggeshall for look at all the
20 antique shops and buy presents and memories.
21 As the sun was still shining we drove in
22 Clacton, a typical british seaside resort,
23 complete with a pier and donkey rides to
24 a kids.
25   Next week we will picking strawberries at
26 Tiptree and go to a Oyster Fishery.
27   Hope you and John are all well.
28   Yours faithfully,
         Ursula

3.2

List an itinerary for your town or a town you know. Use the same headings as the
leaflet. (Day 1 Morning, Afternoon, etc.)

3.3

Write out the itinerary from 3.2 giving as much information as you can about
what there is to do. You are writing a leaflet for tourists. Use photographs,
drawings or pictures, and refer to them in your writing if you want to.

16 I stopped the car and took it . . .

NARRATIVE WRITING

In this unit you will look at different anecdotes (short, interesting, amusing, true stories) and then practise writing your own.

─── **1** ───────────────────────────

Below, there is an anecdote. When people talk or write about themselves, they often do it in the form of an anecdote. This anecdote is true.

1.1

Work in pairs. Read the anecdote and fill in the missing words. More than one answer is sometimes possible.
Example: (a) = I was

(a) .... driving back to Oxford University at the start of the new term.
(b) .... was 1967, times were easy for everybody, the Beatles were at their height and love, peace and Flower Power were in the air. (c) ....
I was a student I wore a pair of old jeans, a football shirt and a secondhand American army jacket.
   (d) .... a road sign at the side of the road. It wasn't attached to anything, anyone could take (e) .... I stopped the car and (f)
....
   (g) .... I was shutting the car door a hand caught my wrist. 'Where do you think you're going with that (h) .... ?' said a deep voice. The (i) .... belonged to a policeman.

1.2

Work in small groups. Read the anecdote in 1.1 again and write an end to the story. Write between two and four paragraphs.

2

Work in small groups. Think of an anecdote that you have told about yourself or about someone you know.

 Make notes about the anecdote first, then tell it to the group.

Then, with your teacher's help, write your anecdote or someone else's. Write about a page. Here are some phrases that can be used to introduce anecdotes:

Phrases

. . . something rather odd happened last week . . .
We had a strange experience on holiday last year . . .
You'll never guess what Fred's just done . . .

3

3.1

Read the short story below and underline the link words (words like *and*, *but*, *so*, *because*, *at first*).

The necklace

(Based on the short story The necklace *by Guy de Maupassant.)*

A very poor woman had an invitation to a party given by a rich friend of hers. At first she thought she couldn't accept the invitation because she had nothing to wear and no jewellery. But then she thought, 'Oh why not! This is the only party I'll go to this year. Maybe it's the only party I'll ever go to.'

 So she made herself a dress from some cloth that somebody gave her. She also borrowed a beautiful necklace from her rich friend. The necklace was the most beautiful thing she had ever seen. At the party she felt rich and beautiful and entirely lifted out of her usual poor, drab world. She laughed, she drank, she danced, she talked, she sparkled and she laughed again.

 She was still laughing when she got home, walking on air. She put her hand up to touch the beautiful necklace and her face froze. The laughter died in her throat. The necklace was gone.

 Next day she went to a jeweller and described the necklace. 'How much,' she asked,' would a necklace like that cost?' The jeweller named a huge amount of money. The woman went to a moneylender and borrowed that amount of money. She bought a new necklace, identical to the one she had lost, and gave it to her rich friend. The friend didn't notice the difference. She took the necklace, put it away in a drawer and forgot about it.

 But the woman had to pay back the moneylender, a little every week, with interest. So she took two jobs, one during the day and one in the evening. At night she took in sewing and repaired people's clothes. That way she could just pay back her weekly amount to the moneylender.

 She worked like that for twenty years. She never married because she never met anybody. She worked eighteen hours a day. At forty she looked sixty, lined and yellow, but she had paid back the loan to the moneylender. Of course, she had lost touch with her rich friend years ago.

One day, however, she met the friend by chance in the street. 'Hello,' said the friend, secretly horrified at how old and ugly the woman had become. The woman asked if the rich friend remembered the party and the necklace.

'Necklace?' said the rich friend.

'You know,' said the woman, 'the necklace I borrowed from you for the party.'

'Oh that!' laughed the rich friend. 'That wasn't a real necklace. It was just an imitation. Just paste. Not worth anything at all.'

3.2

Write all the link words from the story under the categories in the chart below.

+ +	+ (−) − (+)	→
and	but	so

3.3

Work in pairs. Can you think of any more link words that are not in the story? Write them in the correct columns too.

── **4** ─────────────────────────────

Read the story in 3.1 again.

Write a paragraph about how the woman looked for the missing necklace but did not dare tell her rich friend that it was lost. Your paragraph should fit between paragraphs three and four of the story in 3.1. Use the phrases below to help you. Discuss your paragraph with the person next to you before you start writing, if you want to.

Phrases

left tiny room . . .   went back . . .   kept her eyes . . .   looking for . . .   outside friend's . . .   started to cry . . .   no sign of . . .   through the window . . .   rich friend's house . . .   clearing up . . .   party . . .   tell friend . . .   lost necklace? . . .   couldn't . . .   went home . . .   still crying . . .

── **5** ─────────────────────────────

Can you think of a short story, a myth, a film, the plot of a TV series or video that you know? Make notes about it and discuss it in small groups.

Write the story. Write about a page.

17 . . . the 18% pay rise for so-called 'Top People'

WRITING ABOUT PUBLIC EVENTS   I

In this unit you will look at newspaper descriptions of different events, and learn how 'newspaper English' differs from ordinary English. You will then practise writing your own descriptions of different events in ordinary English.

––––– **1** –––––

Change the newspaper articles on the left to ordinary English, using the help given on the right. The underlined words in the newspaper articles are examples of newspaper English.

A

THE LEADER of the opposition, Ron Paynter 41, <u>yesterday condemned</u> as 'totally unacceptable' the 18% pay rise for so-called 'Top People'.

The pay rises, announced by <u>Prime Minister Betty Sims</u> last week, are for senior civil servants, judges and others in leading positions in the country.

The announcement has <u>particularly angered teach</u>ers, who have been offered only 7% <u>in the latest pay round</u>. The main teachers' union, NUT, yesterday threatened strike action when <u>negotiations broke down</u>. The pay rises for Top People are in some cases more than a teacher's entire salary, <u>according to</u> teachers' leader, Brian Beak.

Ron Paynter <u>fully suppor</u>ted the teachers' <u>threatened strike</u> action and said he would talk to pickets who were handing out leaflets at his son's school in Hampstead, London.

Yesterday, Mr Ron Paynter . . .   criticized the 18% . . .   He said . . .

The Prime Minister, . . .
They are for . . .

Teachers . . .   about the announcement because . . .   recent negotiations.   The main . . . failed.   Brian Beak, the teachers' leader, said that . . .

Ron Paynter agreed . . .   He said . . .

B

> **John McGuire, contro-**
> **versial number one rank-**
> **ing tennis star, was**
> **yesterday fined just £20**
> **for spitting at an oppo-**
> **nent at Wimbledon.**
>
> The fine was described
> as 'far too small, a
> disgrace,' by Juan Lopez
> who McGuire spat at
> during an argument
> about a disputed service
> line call.
>
> McGuire called Lopez's
> service out, but the umpire,
> supported by a service
> machine that did not bleep,
> said it was in.
>
> The crowd slow-hand-
> clapped and booed during
> the subsequent row.

You know John McGuire, the tennis player?
He is ranked . . .   always in trouble. I saw
him at Wimbledon last week.
He . . . with another player, Juan Lopez.

The row was about . . .   The service
machine . . .   McGuire said . . .   The
crowd . . .   In the end McGuire spat . . .
   I read in the paper that McGuire . . .
yesterday. Lopez said . . .   He said it
was . . .

2

2.1

The words and phrases below are from four different parts of an English newspaper. Which word or phrase goes in which part of the newspaper?

Parts of a newspaper

1 *Sport*   2 *Home news*   3 *Foreign news*   4 *The arts*

Words and phrases

a)   a plane crash in Japan
b)   won a gold medal
c)   the House of Commons
d)   an excellent review
e)   his latest film
f)   a bomb has exploded in London
g)   bank robbery in Leicester
h)   won in three sets
i)   the New York subway strike

j)   aid for the famine areas
k)   off form
l)   an Oscar
m)   a government enquiry
n)   local trains are running late
o)   the French franc is up 3%
p)   won the match
q)   the terrorists were arrested in London

2.2

Work in pairs. Below there are some personal reactions to public events. Add a personal reaction to the words and phrases in 2.1 and write sentences. You will need to add words that are not in the words and phrases list or the personal reactions list.

Example:

From Words and phrases (2.1)	From Personal reactions (below)
There was a plane crash in Japan.	It was terrible.

Personal reactions

I'm delighted
terrible/horrible
It serves them right
I think he/she was / they were lucky
disgraceful
I don't know how they get away with it

I'm glad it's finished
When is the government going to do
  something about it?
It's about time.
He/she deserves / they deserve it

3

Take one of the sentences you wrote in 2.2 and, with the help of your teacher and the rest of the class, tell a story with that sentence in it. Then write the story. Write two or three paragraphs.

4

Work in small groups. Read the three newspaper stories and choose one of them to work on.

In your groups, discuss what could happen next in the story you have chosen, and what you think happened in the end. Take notes on the group discussion if you want to.

In your own words, continue the story in writing, and write an end to the story. Imagine that this is part of a letter to a friend about a newspaper story that interested you. Write between two and four paragraphs.

A FOURTEEN-year-old Brian Fitzpatrick has just asked his parents to leave home. And they may have to go, because Brian paid for the family house.

Two years ago whiz-kid Brian thought of a new computer game. He sold it to Magna Computers plc and so far it has made him £250,000.

B LOCAL milkman Bernard Cornwell was sacked yesterday for wearing shorts while he delivered the milk.

A spokesman for Bernard's company 'Coronation Milk' said, 'Mr Cornwell has been warned twice. His shorts are too short.'

But all is not lost for the milkman with the bare legs. Local housewives are organizing a petition demanding his reinstatement.

C HEART transplant patient Phil Green wants to sail solo across the Atlantic in a 20 foot boat to raise money for heart transplants.

But a leading heart specialist, Dr Raymond Morgan of Queen's Hospital, Leeds, yesterday appealed to him to call it off.

'It's too soon after his operation,' said Dr Morgan.

18 . . . local people have started a petition

WRITING ABOUT PUBLIC EVENTS   II

This unit will help you understand how link words are used. You will then
continue to practise writing descriptions of different events.

── 1 ─────────────────────────────

1.1

Here are three mixed up stories about world record attempts. Write one of them
as a paragraph in less than five minutes.

This week there was an attempt to break the world record for	a) crossing the Atlantic in a power boat. b long distance flying in a hot air balloon. c) climbing the most Alpine mountains in a week.	a) Chris Hetherington, who has led several expeditions in the Himalayas, b) The crew of the 'Blue Wave' are all experienced sailors. c) Three students from Cambridge are taking their pet dog with them into the clouds.
a) One of the trio apparently said that the animal doesn't mind heights as long as it doesn't rain. b) is someone I admire a great deal. c) Their attempt is being sponsored by AFB, who make nautical equipment and boats, among other things.	a) I suppose they want the publicity, and nobody asked the crew to risk their lives. b) I thought that was rather funny, c) I think he's got a lot of courage,	a) but I hope he hasn't bitten off more than he can chew this time b) But something about these 'stunt' world record attempts still worries me. c) but I hope he still likes heights when he comes down from the clouds!
a) I mean, the total cost of all this 'fun and games' on the water	a) It all looked so ridiculous on telly last night! b) is over £250,000.	a) A real contribution to Britain's achievement in this field.

»»→

63

b) Apparently they are taking champagne and strawberries and cream up there with them.

c) because he's pushing fifty now.

You could build a hospital or a school for that.

c) Still, it would be marvellous if he could do it.

b) They were even making the dog wave its paw as they disappeared out of sight.

c) And there have been dozens of record attempts like this. The public is bored with them.

1.2

Underline the link words that helped you to put the story together.

1.3

Pick out words, phrases or sentences that show the author's attitude.

2

Work in pairs. Using the flow chart below, write a report about a state visit to your country.

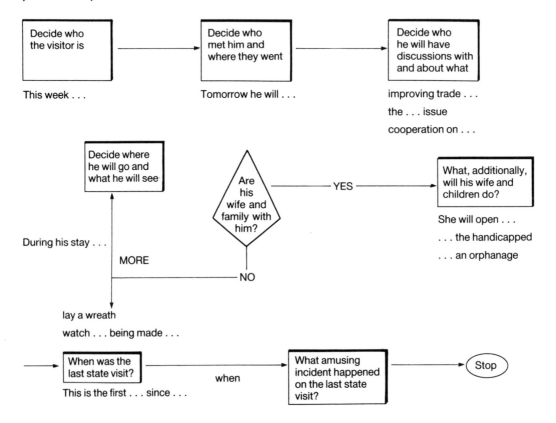

─── **3** ───────────────────────────

3.1

Read the newspaper report of a train crash below. In pairs, change the seven underlined examples of newspaper English to the kind of English you would write in a letter. Then, in your own words, write about the train crash in a letter to a friend. Write one paragraph only.

A HIGH speed train crashed into a stationary goods train last night, killing two people and injuring another three. The injured were taken to the John Radcliffe Hospital in Oxford.

The train, the 11 o'clock from Paddington to Oxford, was (1) believed to be out of control when the accident (2) occurred. (3) Early reports indicate that the driver had a heart attack. Many passengers were thrown clear on impact or (4) the number of casualties would have been higher.

One of the first people on the scene was Mrs Frances Bradshaw (4) of Derby Street, Headington. Mrs Bradshaw, who is trained in First Aid, was later (6) commended by the police for her prompt treatment of the injured.

Another Headington resident, Stephen Buckley, (7) 29, of Duke Avenue, pulled several people clear of the wreckage.

This is the third train crash on this part of the line in six months. Local people have started a petition asking British Rail to investigate the crashes. Both Stephen Buckley and Frances Bradshaw have signed the petition.

3.2 ▭

Listen to the radio interview about the same train crash and note down the differences from the newspaper report. There are seven differences.

3.3

Using the paragraph you wrote in 3.1 to help you, write about the radio interview about the train crash in your own words. Again, imagine you are writing a letter to a friend about a public event that interested you.

SECTION 5: EXTENSIVE WRITING — EVALUATION AND OPINION

19 I love Elvis – but the show never came alive

EVALUATION IN WRITING

In this unit you will think about plays, films, TV programmes and books, and consider your opinion of them, before looking at the kind of language used to describe them, and writing your own evaluations.

Note

You will need to prepare Exercises 1 and 4 in advance.

—— **1** ————————————————————————————

1.1

Write a quiz (ten questions) about books, theatre, TV and films. Either use your own knowledge or ask people outside your class for questions, or look up the questions in a reference book. You must be able to answer your own quiz questions. Use the questions below to give you ideas.

Questions

With a question word
What do . . . and . . . have in
    common?
Where does . . . live in the film/book/
    play . . . ?
In the play . . . what did . . . do?
In the film/TV programme . . .
    where did . . . live/work?

Without a question word
Who wrote . . . ?
Who was the star of . . . ?
Who plays . . . in . . . ?
What nationality is . . . ?
Where are . . . set?
Who directed / starred in . . . ?
Which novel . . . ?

1.2

In pairs, write the answers to someone else's quiz questions.

2

Work in pairs. First find all the words and phrases listed below that refer to a
whole play (like 'hopeless') and not just part of it (like 'the acting was superb').
Then put the adjectives and adverbs in order of strength (for example, 'excellent'
is stronger than 'good'). Now write the words and phrases in two columns in
order of strength. Words and phrases referring to the whole play, with strong
adjectives and adverbs should come first.

totally convincing, hopeless, full of clichés, very moving, the plot
was incredibly bad, magnificently shot, the characters were
inconsistent, the acting was superb, banal, the characterization was
poor, an excellent production, believable, X played the part of Y
well, terrible, the story was unbelievable, the plot developed slowly,
obvious, the character development was good, quite moving,
hilariously funny, the set was beautiful.

Praise	*Criticism*
an excellent production	*hopeless*

3

Look at these successes and failures (taken from *The Book of Heroic Failures* and
The Guinness Book of Records).

The Most Oscars
★ Walt Disney, 20
Actors and actresses:
★ Katharine Hepburn, 4
Films:
★ Ben Hur (1959), 11
★ Gone With the Wind (1939), 10
★ West Side Story (1961), 10

Best TV Watchers
★ The American public
Estimated watching per household: 7 hours 2 minutes
per day (1983).
    The average child in the USA has watched 710 days
(17,040 hours) of TV, seen more than 350,000
commercials and more than 15,000 TV murders by the
time he or she is eighteen (estimate).

The Worst Review
At the Duchess Theatre in
London at the turn of the
century there opened a
show called 'A Good
Time'. Next morning it
got the simple review:
'NO'.

The Worst Prop
In 1876 Wagner ordered a
dragon to be made for the
Bayreuth premiere of his opera
'Siegfried'. It was decided to
send it over in sections. The
tail arrived promptly, but then
nothing was seen of the rest of
the dragon for some weeks.
Just as Wagner was losing all
hope, a parcel arrived contain-
ing the torso. However, come
the dress rehearsal, there was
no sign of the dragon's front
end. At last the head came but
minus the neck.
    For the first night the head
had to be joined straight on to
the body with the result that
critics found the animal an
endless source of merriment.
The neck never arrived.
    It was said later that a clerk
had in error sent it not to
Bayreuth in Germany but to
Beirut, capital of Lebanon.

⫸→

Longest Running TV Series

★ Tora San films
From August 1968 to 1983 in Japan.

The Worst Mishap in a Stage Production

There were historic scenes at the first and last night of 'Ecarte' in London in 1870. The play was laughed off the stage before the end.

Its failure was almost certainly due to a picnic scene early in the course of the play for which, out of generosity and a concern for realism whole roast chickens, pies, and an unlimited supply of real champagne was provided.

The cast drank freely and there was much joking amongst them, which was quite inaudible to the audience. Soon the actors were laughing, bumping into the props and leaning against the scenery. Then the male lead started shouting all his lines and kept this up until he appeared to go to sleep.

Most Expensive Film

★ Star Trek, world premiere Washington D.C., 6 December 1979.
Director: Robert Wise,
Producer: Gene Roddenberry,
Cost: $46 million.

Highest Number of Takes

★ 28 by the comedy actress Pat Coombs in a TV commercial.
Said Ms Coombs, 'Every time we came to the punch line I just could not remember the name of the product.'

Highest Box Office Gross

★ Gone With the Wind (1939)
Stars: Clark Gable, Vivien Leigh.
Took $312 million.

Make notes about the best or worst film, TV programme, play or book you have ever seen or read.

Read your notes to someone else in the class or your teacher.

Working from your notes, write three or four paragraphs about the film, TV programme, play or book.

―― **4** ――――――――――――――――――――――――――――――

(*Before the lesson.*) With your teacher and the rest of the class, choose a TV play
or a TV series episode that you want to watch and then discuss (it must be fiction).

  With your teacher and the rest of the class, choose three members of the class to
give presentations (short talks) on three aspects of the programme (see
presentation notes below).

  After the three presentations, have a class discussion of the programme with
your teacher. During your discussion you will want to evaluate what you have
seen, and these phrases may help you. On the left there are some informal
evaluation phrases, and on the right some phrases for interruption in a discussion
about plays, films or novels.

Phrases

Informal evaluation	*Interruption*
I loved it	That reminds me of . . .
I was bored stiff	Yes, that happened in . . .
It was awful	It was quite different in . . .
It was absolutely marvellous	Well, I'm not sure about that . . .
I couldn't get through it (*for books*)	Yes, but . . .

After the discussion, write at least a page about the programme. Describe and
evaluate it.

――

Presentation notes

Note   If you are watching the programme in your own language do not try to
translate dialogue directly. Give a general idea in English of what the characters
said.

Presentation 1	*Presentation 2*	*Presentation 3*
Tell the group everything that happened in the programme.	Choose an important character and say what happened from that character's point of view. Use the first person (I . . .)	Evaluate the programme. Was it good or bad? Why?

―――― **5** 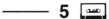 ――――――――――――――――――――――――

Here are some phrases to evaluate music.

Phrases

Positive	*Negative*
very moving . . .	discordant . . .
beautiful . . .	sounds awful . . .
lyrical . . .	I couldn't concentrate on it . . .
really peaceful . . .	

Listen to the cassette. Imagine that you were given a cassette or an LP of each of these pieces of music as a birthday present. How would you feel about it and why?

Write your impressions of and response to each piece of music. Compare your impressions and response with the person next to you.

20 The old idea that every woman needs a man is on the way out

OPINION IN WRITING

In this unit you will consider various subjects, including crime and marriage, and write your own opinions about them.

—— **1** ——

Which of these are opinions? What are the others?

a) The divorce rate is higher than before, but in my view that does not mean that marriage is weaker, just that people are demanding more from it.
b) Crimes of violence increased by 4% last year.
c) Personally, I think that people will no longer have just one career. In the future they may well have three or four.
d) Serial marriage means marrying one person, divorcing them, then marrying another and divorcing them and so on.
e) For example, if there are three serial marriages the first could be for romance, the second for partnership and the third for companionship in old age.
f) The crime rate is going up. It's shocking. You only have to open the paper and there's another terrible story.
g) The trend since the war tells us more than the statistics for any one year.
h) The sentence for crimes against the person, especially rape, should be higher and, arguably, the sentence for crimes against property could be reduced.
i) If people took the trouble to fit stronger locks to their doors and windows there would be fewer burglaries.
j) I would bring back the death penalty, I really would.
k) Far more women these days live alone and have successful careers. The old idea that every woman needs a man is on the way out.
l) Politically, there will be a return to the centre. People are tired of swings to the right and then the left and then back again.

2

Work in groups. Below, there are two quotations about the future. There are also some phrases for expressing opinion.

2.1

Discuss the quotations with the others in your group.

Quotations	*Phrases*
'Russia will certainly inherit the future.' (*D.H. Lawrence*) 'The future is . . . black.' (*James Baldwin*)	I agree/disagree with . . . . . . completely correct . . . . . . wrong . . . In my opinion/view . . . It seems to me . . .

2.2

Write your opinion of one of the quotations. Use the phrases for expressing opinion to help you. Write two to four paragraphs.

3

3.1

Work in pairs. One of you looks at A and the other looks at B. Practise all the phrases about crime and crime prevention.
Example: A says 'There should be warnings in public places.'
B says 'Right, but posters won't stop pickpockets.'

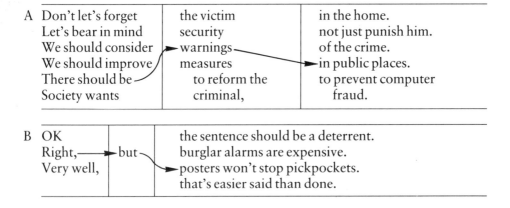

A	Don't let's forget	the victim	in the home.
	Let's bear in mind	security	not just punish him.
	We should consider	warnings	of the crime.
	We should improve	measures	in public places.
	There should be	to reform the	to prevent computer
	Society wants	criminal,	fraud.

B	OK		the sentence should be a deterrent.
	Right,	but	burglar alarms are expensive.
	Very well,		posters won't stop pickpockets.
			that's easier said than done.

3.2

Work in small groups. Discuss how large a fine or how long a prison sentence should be given for the crimes below. For example, should there be a death penalty for murder? Should the sentence for blackmail be more or less than the sentence for rape? Is suicide a crime? *Why* should some crimes carry a heavier sentence?

Complete the chart below and compare your group's fines and sentences with other groups.

Crime	*Fine or sentence of . . .*
soliciting bigamy (attempted) suicide forgery theft destroying or damaging property handling stolen goods murder blackmail performing an obscene play burglary with a firearm possession of drugs rape	

3.3

Write three or four paragraphs about your opinions on sentencing for crime.

Note

The Teacher's Book lists the kind of sentence given for each of these crimes in Britain today. However, in Britain, a judge may decide to give a longer or shorter sentence depending on the circumstances.

4

Listen to the extract from a radio programme on the cassette. Make a note of the opinions you hear on the cassette on these subjects:

The reasons for the increase in crime and how to stop it
Why people turn to drugs and how to stop them
The death penalty for serious crimes

Write down your opinion on each subject. In pairs, compare your views with those of the people on the cassette.

—— **5** ————————————————————————

5.1

Look at these headlines about marriage. They are all from *The Times*. Guess what the stories could be about. (The answers are in the Teacher's Book.)

Headlines

A # Bride dies hours after hospital wedding

B
American women are branching out into big business

Missionaries of womenpower spread the success gospel

C # Declarations of independence

More and more people are choosing to live alone.
What is the singular attraction?

D ## Politicians and happy marriages

5.2

Choose two of the stories and discuss them with your teacher and the class.

5.3

Write your opinion of the issues in the stories.

To the teacher

Scope and dimensions of the book

Level

This is a twenty unit intermediate writing skills book. It is suitable for learners who have had from 150 class hours of English to intermediate learners with five or six years of English.

Gradation

There is gradation of difficulty from Unit 1 to Unit 20 which accommodates the span of learner ability indicated above.

Length of units

The twenty units in the Learner's Book average two or three class hours each, depending on how much of the writing is done in class. Sometimes additional tasks are suggested in the Teacher's Book and if these are introduced more time must be allowed. In the longer units some exercises are marked with an asterisk (*). These can be omitted if there is time pressure, or done as homework.

Order of units

The units are independent of each other, so it is possible to leave some units out and do others more intensively, developing all the ideas in the Teacher's Book and in this Introduction. It is also possible to vary the order of units.

Suggested teaching techniques

The transfer from oral/aural to written work

Although the traditional text is one stimulus to written work, there are several others and oral/aural work in pairs or groups or as a full class is one of them. These activities require the learners to perform a task orally/aurally first, the teacher adds input, then the learners perform the task in writing.
 The stages from oral/aural to written work are as follows:
1 Learners carry out the oral/aural task in the exercise.
2 Teacher monitors language using a Feedback Sheet.

A Feedback Sheet looks like this.

You said	You should have said	This was interesting

Write learner errors in the *You said* column. Write correct utterances and anything useful the learners could have said but did not in the *This was interesting* column. If the oral/aural work is done as a full class, learners will soon get used to you writing on a Feedback Sheet while they speak (especially if the feedback is mainly positive). If the oral/aural work is done in pairs or small groups they will soon get used to you going round jotting items down.

3 When the oral/aural work is finished you and the learners together correct errors and they write the correct version in the *You should have said* column. Ideally, photocopy the Feedback Sheet for the learners immediately, but you could copy the Feedback Sheet on to the board or an OHP.

4 You and the learners then plan the writing task set in the exercise. You can do this at three levels of support:

Level 1

You and the class do the writing task orally and you write it on the board. You draw the learners' attention to features of language they were getting wrong in the oral/aural phase. When your board writing is complete you cloze it (make gaps by deleting every fifth or seventh word). The better the learners the more gaps you leave. They then write the paragraph, filling in the gaps you left. This considerable degree of support is useful for weak classes writing not more than one paragraph.

Level 2

You and the learners do the writing task orally and you make notes on the board. You write key items of vocabulary and suggest link words like 'however', 'so', 'but'.

Level 3

You write only key vocabulary items on the board.

Notemaking

Notemaking is learners making notes on their own views and experiences (as opposed to notetaking which is from an exterior source like a text or cassette). Learners can make notes before they begin any piece of writing.

However, notemaking really comes into its own when learners are writing two or three paragraphs or more. Learners then make notes before they start writing and hand the notes in as a Writing Plan. The teacher then corrects aspects like the logical ordering of material, paragraphing and linking between paragraphs before learners start to write. This leaves the teacher free to concentrate on sentence level language errors when the writing is handed in.

Error correction

Here are some suggestions for correcting written work:

1 Correct the errors in the written work and give the work back to the learners. Ask if they have any questions about your corrections. Possibly ask them to rewrite incorrect sentences correctly.
2 Go round correcting learners' work in class as they are writing.
3 Underline the errors on learners' written work but do not correct them. Draw up a Feedback Sheet. A Feedback Sheet for learners' written errors looks like this:

You wrote	You should have written	Why
I have told him yesterday	*I told him yesterday*	*Tense*

Copy a representative sample of learners' errors (not all of them) on to the *You wrote* column of the Feedback Sheet. Photocopy the Feedback Sheet so each learner has a copy. In class, you and the learners correct the errors and the learners write the correction in the *You should have written* column. You and the learners classify each of the errors in the *Why* column. For example, the error might be Tense, Preposition, Subject–Verb agreement and so on. You will need a 'miscellaneous' category like Wrong Phrase to cover semantic errors.

When you have used this kind of Feedback Sheet three or four times you and the learners together decide which error categories are coming up most often. You and the learners might like to decide together on a numbering system for the error categories. For example, Tense could be 1, Articles could be 2, Wrong Phrase could be 3, and so on. Do not have more than nine categories, including the miscellaneous 'catch all' category of Wrong Phrase.

Next time you use a Feedback Sheet for written errors use the numbering system that you and the learners devised.

Learners should correct the errors you underlined on their own written work as well as correcting the errors on the Feedback Sheet. However, instead of learners correcting after each homework you could have a correction session in class, after, say, three homeworks. At the correction session learners correct the errors you underlined with reference to the Feedback Sheets that you and they filled in. Learners could also put the error number in the margin, using the numbering system you and the learners have devised.

4 Underline the errors in the learners' work *or* write the number of errors the learner made at the bottom of the page.

In class, learners in small groups correct the errors in pencil. Take the work in again and check the corrections. This technique works best for short pieces of work, of paragraph length or less. It is particularly useful in mixed ability groups.

5 This is a variant of 4 (above). Underline the errors in the learners' work *or* write the number of errors the learner made at the bottom of the page.

In class, learners in small groups correct the errors in pencil. Each small group is responsible for one type of error only (for example, Tense or Preposition or Wrong Phrase). Learners' work is passed from group to group, so as many types of error as possible are looked for and corrected.

6 Learners in pairs correct each other's work before you have seen it. They can correct each other after every paragraph or after they have finished writing. Then take the work in and correct both the work and the learners' corrections.

7 When learners have finished writing in class, a learner, or two or three learners, copy their writing on to the board and you and the class correct it, sentence by sentence. This is clearly for work of paragraph length or less.

In my opinion all these correction techniques should be used, but 3, which is the most thorough, is time consuming and can only be used occasionally.

Upgrading

Upgrading is helping the learners to rewrite their work at a level more like a native speaker. This important technique not only raises the level of learners' English but helps them to develop an intuition, a 'feel' for the language.

Upgrading is concerned not with language error but with grammatically correct language that would not sound natural to a native speaker. It is concerned with features like over-simple language, incorrect selection of material, incorrect prioritization of information and viewpoint, incorrect thematization (making the wrong thing the subject of the sentence), failure to state or restate the subject of a sentence, misunderstanding the social implications of language (for example 'I want' instead of 'I would like'), misusing idiom or using idiom too little or too much, and incorrect or fluctuating register (too formal or too informal).

Only some of these categories can be made overt to intermediate learners. However, learners should be told to watch out for language that is rude or over-polite, too formal or too informal and too simple. The word 'unnatural' will have to cover the other categories above.

Steps in upgrading are as follows:

1 Make it clear to the learners that they will be asked to rewrite work produced by a different member of the class from time to time. This is an inevitable part of raising the level of their English and does not mean the work was unsatisfactory. Ideally, each learner in the class should have his or her work upgraded once during the year.

2 Put a corrected piece of written work on an OHP (the board will do) and ask for further improvements. You will have to do nearly all of the upgrading yourself. So upgrade the work, sentence by sentence, until it is at or nearer native-speaker level. Let one or two learners read it aloud to get the feel of it. Then they copy it down, preferably with a time limit.

3 Learners keep upgraded work as a model and ideally should refer to it from time to time.

Another way of upgrading is to work with the learners while they are writing in class.

Recycling

Recycling is using the learners' own work as a stimulus to further writing. Learners read the corrected version of another learner's letter, for example, and then reply to it.

If you are doing one of the units intensively there is plenty of opportunity for recycling, especially among the personal letters.

Symbols

 = Cassette

* = The exercise can be omitted or done as homework (only marked in the Teacher's Book).

Acknowledgements

The author and publishers are grateful to the authors, publishers and others who have given permission for the use of copyright material identified in the text. It has not been possible to identify the sources of all the material used and in such cases the publishers would welcome information from copyright owners.

Waltham Forest Recreation Services for the extract from the 'Out of work' leaflet on p. 2; the Office of Fair Trading for 'Making your complaint' on p. 41; International Biographical Centre for the extract about Sophia Loren from *The World Who's Who of Women* on p. 45; Andre Deutsch for the extract from *How to be Seventy* by George Mikes on p. 45(c); Colchester Caravanning and Camping Park Ltd for the leaflet about Colchester on p. 55; Futura Publications for the extracts from *The Book of Heroic Failures* by Stephen Pile and Guinness Superlatives Ltd for the extracts from *The Guinness Book of Records* (1985) on pp. 67–8.

Photographs on pp. 29 and 46 by Nigel Luckhurst; on p. 46 by David Runnacles; on p.52 (a) by Travel Photo International; (b) and (c) by James Davis photography; (d) by David Horwell; (e) from the Society for Cultural Relations with the USSR; (f) by Koene/Colorific!
Illustrations by Clyde Pearson on pp. 10, 11, 39, 46, 47; by Leslie Marshall on pp. 15 and 16. Artwork by Wenham Arts and Ace Art.

Book design by Peter Ducker MSTD